Comments From Listeners

"Tony Mayo covers a lot of meaningful ground in a handful of pages - he brings together courage, bravery, belonging, acceptance, compassion and more—and backs it up with insights, experience, AND academic references! I loved it!" – Ron Dimon, author of *EPM Done Right* (Wiley CIO Series)

"I am moved and inspired. It is absolutely great, challenging, and rich. Plus, more adjectives are in me—all superlative, I'm sure. I must listen to it at least 2 more times; there is a lot to grok here." – Lowell Nerenberg, Executive Coach

"Thank you Tony, for such a wonderful message this morning. It was so uplifting and based on feedback, provided many with a transformational experience."
– Email from UUCR Board member

"Tony, one of the things I valued most about your sermon is that so few words were wasted. You did not speak just to fill the time; each sentence added to the whole." – Email from UUCR Member

---

"Tony, I have it on good authority that your sermon this last Sunday was about the best ever. Could I get a printed copy?" – Email from church member who had been out of town.

"We were inspired by what you shared and how you shared it. Thank you." – Email from Guest at Service

---

"I so appreciate your wonderful talk yesterday morning. A great reminder for me to continue to take risks in my life and get out of my comfort zone as well as trusting others. It also reminded me of the importance of meditation in my life." – Email from UUCR Member

"Your message was loud and clear and magically delivered. Thank you." – Email from UUCR Member

"Please let me know when you have a written version to share. My life could use more Courage just now, and your talk gave me some ideas that could help." – Email from UUCR Member

"I found your sermon to be rich and meaningful. I agree that you should make it available in print. I would like to revisit it, and those who missed it should take a look!" – Email from UUCR Member

"True courage comes from the heart.

"I was fortunate enough to hear this sermon in real life and was glad to see that Tony has put it in writing so it will be easy to share. I love his distinction between courage that comes from the heart and bravery (related to bravado) that is put on like armor to conceal weakness. He encouraged us to live authentic lives, risking vulnerability as we act from our true selves. I need to revisit what he shared with us on that memorable Sunday!" – Laurie Dodd, Attorney

"It's rare that I find something so uplifting and encouraging. I am not a religious person and usually when I hear the word 'sermon' I run. His message is for everyone and stays clear of religious views that might preclude any person or group from understanding and enjoying what he has to share.
"Tony has a wonderful way with words. I highly recommend reading this book or finding the audio version."
– Michael Cohen

"Not a sermon, but rather an invitation.
"Though this piece was delivered as a sermon, it is a compelling, intellectual essay on that least intellectual piece of us, our hearts. Tony makes it clear that if we're going to feel fulfilled, connected and alive, we're going to have to reveal our hearts."
– Robert "Rohit" Millstein, Investment Manager

Please post your review on Amazon at:
http://tiny.cc/TonySermon

Contents

Preface — xi

Part One

Musical Introduction — 3
Being Ourselves Together — 5

Part Two

Musical Transition — 19
The Courage to be in Community — 21

Part Three

How to BE in Courageous,
Genuine Relationships — 43

About the Author — 63
Before you go ... — 65

How do we balance
the universal human needs
of authenticity and acceptance
in our personal lives?

How might we foster communities
where others have the courage
to be truly themselves with us?

Preface

The following is a combined and expanded record of a sermon delivered by Tony Mayo at the Unitarian Universalist Church in Reston on Sunday, January 26, 2014 at the 9:00 and 11:00 a.m. services.

Part One, Time for All Ages: Being Ourselves Together, was delivered with Tony sitting cross-legged on the floor, surrounded by a small group of enthusiastic three to ten year olds. After some songs and ceremony, Tony delivered *Part Two*, his sermon for the adults, titled, *The Courage to be in Community*.

Note on Format

Part One includes words spoken by Tony and responses from the children. It is written in the style of a play, with the name of the speaker on the left and the dialogue on the right.

Part Two is in familiar paragraph form. The text includes cues for the speaker, employing **boldface** to call for verbal emphasis of a word or phrase and ellipses (...) to indicate a silent pause for reflection. The transcriptionists of the original recording included bracketed indications of the congregation's responses, mainly of [laughter]. Feel free to treat these notations as descriptive, not prescriptive.

Part One

Time for All Ages

Musical Introduction

Choir Master sings *Brave*,
by Sara Bareilles and Jack Antonoff, 2013.
http://goo.gl/CHwHeo

I just wanna see you
I wanna see you be brave

Being Ourselves Together

Tony Mayo: I'd like to invite the youngest members of our congregation to come up front with me and have a seat. Today we're going to talk about what I think are some of your favorite movies.

If someone is too shy and wants to bring his parents, that's fine. Any more youngsters who want to come up here with us? Thank you so much.

I know there are a lot of foods you probably like. It might even include a few fruits. How about that round, shiny one? Usually red …

Child: Apple?

Tony Mayo: Apples! Anyone else here like apples?

What do you call that part of the apple, deep inside, that you don't eat?

Child: Seeds!

Tony Mayo: Yes. You could take the seed and grow more apples, right? Inside that seed is all of its "appleness." [Laughter]

The seed is wrapped in, what?

Children: The core.

Tony Mayo: The core, yes, deep inside that apple is the core.

You know, we have a place deep inside, right? It's where we feel a lot of things, our biggest thoughts and plans, our love for the people we care about most, and all the things that matter most to us. What is that part of your body, deep inside here? It's not the tonsils. The "thumpa-thumpa"?

Child: The heart?

Tony Mayo: The heart!

Now, this is interesting. In a lot of languages, languages some of you speak at home, the word for heart is *cour*. It's the same word. It's the core or heart of something. We get some other important words from this word *cour*—discord & accord. The one I want us to talk about today is cour-age.

Do you know what courage means? What's courage?

Child: It's ... I don't know.

Tony Mayo: It's a hard one to explain, isn't it? I think it means to do something that you know in your heart is right, something you feel is right even if it seems hard.

Have you done anything that's courageous?

How about raising your hand even when you're not sure of the answer? That's courageous, to just give answering a try. What about being up here in front of everybody; that's something. If you follow your heart, that's courage.

It's not a coincidence that these are all the same words.

The other day I saw a movie that I liked a lot. I don't know if it's the sort of thing you would like because it is silly, has lots of singing and dancing. It's about a little penguin. All of its friends and family sing, but this little penguin doesn't sing. Do you know this movie?

Child: Happy Feet

Tony Mayo: Right, Happy Feet. Why do they call it Happy Feet? Because Mumble dances instead of singing. He couldn't sing so they called him Mumble. Just like me, Mumble couldn't sing, but he could dance. When everybody found out that he dances but did not sing, they were 'thrilled' with this, right? ... How'd that go over with his family?

Child: They didn't like it.

Tony Mayo: They didn't like it. Do you remember

how the movie turned out?

Mumble got such a bad response to his need to dance, to express what's in his core, that he actually left his community. He was captured by humans and was trapped in a sort of zoo for a while. Do you remember how he got out?

Child: Dancing.

Tony Mayo: Yes! He was a great dancer. Mumble couldn't sing, just like me. I can't dance either. Luckily, I can talk. [Laughter]

He started dancing in his enclosure, and the people realized he was special, so they let him go and followed Mumble all the way back home, just in time for the humans to help the penguin colony. It turned out that his dancing is what saved the whole community. After that, other penguins in his community started to learn to dance as well as sing. That was the end of the movie.

This kind of story, where someone doesn't fit in, and the others don't like her, but finally the thing that made her different is exactly what saves the day later on. You see this sort of thing quite a bit in stories for children, right?

What about Rudolph? What was Rudolph's problem?

Child: He had a shiny nose.

Tony Mayo: That didn't go over so big, did it? They wouldn't play with him. How'd that one turn out? What did Rudolph do?

Child: He saved Christmas.

Tony Mayo: He saved Christmas. His strange, shiny nose became the very thing Santa needed to find his way to everyone's home on Christmas Eve.

Luke Skywalker – in the beginning of the movie – what was Luke Skywalker doing in Star Wars?

Child: Luke was a farmer.

Tony Mayo: Yeah, Luke was a farmer, but what was Luke at his core, in his heart? Was he a farmer?

He was a Jedi Knight! He finally found that out, left farming to train as a warrior, and he saved the world.

There are a lot of movies like this, right? Mulan, Brave. Wreck it Ralph, Ratatouille, Napoleon Dynamite. You could think of others.

There's something else about these stories. Not only is there someone who is special, who doesn't quite fit in, there is also someone who believes in them. Luke had Obi Wan and Yoda. Finally, the hero embraces the thing that made him different and does something to help everyone.

Mumble had The Amigos, which means The Friends. That makes sense, because that is what true friends do for us, right?

Who knows the word for that thing your friends do for you when you need to do something hard or scary?

They encourage you. *Encourage*

sounds exactly like what it means. Friends put courage in us when we need it!

I'm not sure why there are so many movies on this theme because I'm not a movie producer. I don't know for sure but I have a good guess.

These stories are told to encourage you to do something that is very important and also very hard. Becoming your unique self, acting on what is in your heart, is a vital part of growing up -- but it can be very difficult and frightening to bring that out to the people around you and for those people to accept it in you ...

We're going to do one more thing about courage before you go. We're going to do a part of the Sunday service that normally we do after you've gone downstairs. Today, I want you to stay here and help me with it.

This part of the service is the call and response. I'll say some words and then everybody responds.

	It's not written in your hymnals because your response is simple. It's "Courage!" But you have to say it a particular way. Anybody heard of indoor voices and outdoor voices?
Child:	Yeah, we have to use our outdoor voices?
Tony Mayo:	Outdoor voices! Plus, I want you to push the first part of the word really hard, like this, "KOUR- age." Can you say it that way? Say "KOUR- age!"
All:	COUR-age!
Tony Mayo:	Pretty good. Maybe a little louder.
All:	COUR-age!
Tony Mayo:	What makes a king out of a slave?
All:	COUR-age!
Tony Mayo:	What makes the flag on the mast to wave?
All:	COUR-age!
Tony Mayo:	What makes the elephant charge his

	tusk in the misty mist, or the dusky dusk?
All:	COUR-age!
Tony Mayo:	What makes the muskrat guard his musk?
All:	COUR-age!
Tony Mayo:	What makes the sphinx the seventh wonder?
All:	COUR-age!
Tony Mayo:	What makes the dawn come up like thun-n-n-der?
All:	COUR-age!
Tony Mayo:	What makes the Hottentot so hot?
All:	COUR-age!
Tony Mayo:	What puts the "ape" in apricot?
All:	COUR-age!
Tony Mayo:	What makes you give it all you've got?

All: COUR-age!

Tony Mayo: I just wanted to hear you say that again.
Thank you for your help.
Thank you so much ...

From MGM's *The Wizard of Oz,* 1939
http://goo.gl/P1Zx4K

Part Two

Sermon

Musical Transition

Choir and congregation sing
Cyndi Lauper's 1986 hit, *True Colors*
by Billy Steinberg and Tom Kelly.
http://goo.gl/IStuzN

I see your true colors
Shining through,
I see your true colors
And that's why I love you.

The Courage to be in Community

I'm grateful to be here as part of this community which I joined so recently. I greatly appreciate being trusted with this role in the service, this precious slice of time to talk with you. Of course, with the opportunity comes nervousness. Because I've got something important to me, that matters to me, that I'd like to share and make part of your life ... and I'm cautious of doing something that will hurt my standing in the community. And of course, that is the topic of this sermon.

When our minister asked me to help design a service on the theme of courage, I immediately knew I had to begin with the work of Brené Brown. Professor Brown made a big splash on the Internet with her TED talk and her books are selling very well. She even hit the jackpot; she's been on Oprah more than once. So now this professor of social work is "The Vulnerability Lady."

Vulnerability is a very popular injunction in psychology and self-improvement right now. I was at a conference for executive coaches—that's the work I do—with people from all around the world. At one point, a woman from Holland stood up and said, everyone's talking about being vulnerable and I don't get it. So I went to the dictionary to find out what this English word means and it said vulnerability is, "to make oneself open to attack." Why? Why would I do that? [Laughter]

It's a good question. I'll tell you a little later on the insight I got from the conversation that ensued that day.

But first, take a moment to consider what makes you emotionally vulnerable, feeling like your values could be subject to attack. Maybe there are certain situations, particular people; Parents? People with titles, advanced degrees, or accents? People who deliver sermons? Does asking for something make you feel vulnerable? Or, the opposite, because sometimes to offer seems like another chance to be rejected. Admitting that you're confused, that you're unsure, or it could happen when you're ready to state a firm opinion. Either way, the feeling of emotional vulnerability rises up, we feel it, and it dominates our actions—or our inaction. What are the times when you, in your day-to-day life, feel vulnerable, "open to attack" in some painful, frightening way? Sometimes, this feeling makes you want to withdraw or hide but it is often this very same sense of vulnerability that can make someone angry and aggressive.

As you keep such incidents from your own internal experience in mind, let's exercise our courage, our hearts for a moment, right now, by engaging in a short demonstration together by taking a moment to listen to the inner voice. That voice that's always going even when we're not speaking and there's no one else speaking.

Many people here in the room are experienced meditators; you know this voice very well. On the other hand, if you're one of those people who are thinking, "What voice is he talking about?" I mean the voice that said, "What voice is he talking about?". [Laughter] The "What voice?" voice.

What is that voice saying to you, about you? Things like: Why are we here? How long is it going to take? What good is this demonstration? Am I doing this right, listening correctly? Am I getting the point? Does Tony have a point? ... Look at her; she's doing it right. Oh, there's that guy; I'm doing it better than him ... maybe.

If you pay any attention to this voice, over time you'll notice, as has everyone else I've spoken to about this has, that for most of us most of the time it seems the voice is saying some form of: "Am I good enough? Am I doing it right? Do I deserve to be here? Do – I – belong? Do 'they' recognize that I belong here? Am I ... Acknowledged? Included? Appreciated?" This voice, left to itself, is always doubting, undermining, worrying. Once, I was working on this topic with a group when a participant observed that the mind's screensaver seems to be "Worry."

It's there all the time, *all the time*. Am I good enough ... for ... for what?

To survive? Where we live, especially a place like Reston, survival seems to be handled. We've got food, we've got shelter, crime is low. Our bodies aren't at risk, our life will go on, but there's still this sense of vulnerability, this concern with survival. So what is it that we're protecting? What is this voice continually warning us about if it's not just "staying alive"?

It seems to me that it's **belonging** that's always under attack, that's always vulnerable. Do I deserve to be here? Do they recognize me? Do they appreciate me? Am I included? When I was preparing for this sermon what was difficult for me and surprised me, was how nervous and stressed I felt. That surprised me because, although most people hate the very thought of speaking before a group, for me the fear is the possibility of being in a group and not being allowed to speak. [Laughter]

But I don't want to risk disappointing you, I don't want to lose what acceptance I have, I don't want to screw up an opportunity to give you something valuable. Why do you suppose public speaking is the number one fear? Because it's the perfect opportunity to be rejected by an entire group all in one fell swoop. [Laughter]

I believe there is a great deal of wisdom packed into the language we choose, retained from the origin and changing meanings of common words. Brené Brown pointed out that courage is from the Latin word for heart, *cor*. In early English, courage means, to speak and act on the things closest to your heart, your very core.

After absorbing this insight, my next thought was, "What about bravery?". I thought courage and bravery were synonyms. So I checked the origin of bravery. Bravery is from another Latin word that means *praise*, as in *bravo* or *bravado*.

When you take a word and put the E-R-Y ending on it like livery, upholstery, finery, it means to clothe yourself in materials or images or behaviors. Bravery once meant covering yourself to make you seem worthy of praise. Courage and bravery used to be very different things. We've lost that distinction.

Courage is being true to your heart, your core. Bravery is a cover-up, hiding your true self so that people might respond to the way you'd like to have them think you are.

Since learning this, I've tried to distinguish between the times people around me are being brave versus being courageous. The courageous are encouraged by listening and understanding. The brave appreciate a compassionate friend who makes it safe to drop the armor, to talk about the fear, the pain and doubt, without any risk of losing our relationship, of suddenly not belonging. The brave need to know that I have the same fears. Each of us, you and I, can create a safe space for the expression of our friend's vulnerability by acknowledging our own vulnerability.

But vulnerability is still not quite the right word for today. Vulnerability has become a fairly comfortable, familiar word that we use to talk around and on the surface of something that's much scarier, much uglier. It's what Brené Brown researched for years before she got famous and popular.

Her fundamental topic as a social worker is, the primal fear that fuels our vulnerability. What really threatens our emotional foundations, the survival struggle we all worry about, is called shame.

Shame is the experience of being excluded from a community, of being turned away, of losing the benefits of belonging to a group, perhaps for breaking the often unspoken rules of that culture. Shame, is being pushed out, excluded, and rejected by others. Avoiding shame is a universal human priority. It always has been.

Recognition of this seeming conflict between the yearning to be natural and genuine versus the vital drive to belong, to be accepted, has a long history and a rich vocabulary.

The Classical Greeks had a punishment, that some feared more than death, called ostracizing. Many religious groups use shunning to punish nonconformists and to protect the faithful from exposure to heresy. We all know the story of the Pilgrims who, in words of Garrison Keillor, fled religious persecution in Europe to found a colony in the New World where they would be free to persecute others for their religious beliefs. [Laughter] My home state of Rhode Island was founded by a minister banished from Massachusetts by the Puritans.

In 1872, Charles Darwin wrote a book called *The Expression of the Emotions in Man and Animals*. He noted that in all of the cultures he visited and all the correspondence he received on the topic from around the world, everyone everywhere, when shamed has the same physical response: blushing, mental confusion, downcast eyes, lowered head, slack posture.

Loss of belonging isn't just an emotional threat. It really is a **vital** issue. When, in the mid 1800s, we learned that bacteria are major causes of disease and death, and that there were some materials, antiseptics, that kill off these bacteria, we had sort of an antiseptic craze. It was a fad in the medical world. So much so that the modern, better financed orphanages were designed so that each child had its own crib with clean linen. The orphans were not allowed to interact with the other children. And even when they were fed and cleaned, the staff was told not to handle the children any more than absolutely necessary for fear of passing on a germ.

What happens to infants who are so well protected from infection that they are never kissed or caressed? Some of you have probably heard about this; 60% died within a year. Not just lonely. Not merely unhappy. Not only emotionally deprived, but literally unable to survive. Our desire to belong is a life and death concern. It's not a weakness or personal failure.

We've learned from this experience, of course, and from the courageous work of Harry Harlow in the 1950s with Rhesus monkeys. You may remember seeing photos in your psychology textbook of monkey babies clinging to surrogate mothers made of carpet or wire mesh. He proved—hard as it is to believe that this needed proving—that mother love in the form of physical affection matters to infants. Now preemies are handled in the incubator even though it comes with the risk of infection. We've learned ... but we still have a long way to go.

I heard a radio story a while ago about an office in the government of Los Angeles whose role it is to step in when someone dies who has no next of kin, no one who claims their remains and belongings. These civil servants search for anyone who knows this person, anyone who communicated with the deceased. If there's no one, they clean out the apartment and sell or throw away what's there. Once a year they cremate all these unclaimed bodies and bury them together in a mass grave. Just in L.A., about 3,000 people every year die alone.

People in your neighborhood are not just dying alone, some are dying *because* they feel alone. At my alma mater, the University of Chicago, psychology professor John Cacioppo is doing important and compassionate work on our modern culture's epidemic of loneliness. Just a few days ago, he published research demonstrating that loneliness in the elderly increases the death rate more than obesity and almost as much as being poor.[1]

---

[1] AAAS 2014: *Loneliness is a major health risk for older adults* (Obesity +10%, Loneliness +14%, Poverty +19%) http://goo.gl/ISrH6Q

I'm going to read to you something from Professor Brené Brown's book,

> *The Gifts of Imperfection:*
> *Let Go of Who You Think*
> *You're Supposed to be*
> *and Embrace Who You Are*
> http://goo.gl/GpVgjx

"After collecting thousands of stories, I'm willing to call this a fact: A deep sense of love and belonging is an irreducible need of all women, men, and children. We are biologically, cognitively, physically, and spiritually wired to love, to be loved, and to belong. When those needs are not met, we don't function as we were meant to. We break. We fall apart. We numb. We ache. We hurt others. We get sick. There are certainly other causes of illness, numbing, and hurt, but the absence of love and belonging will always lead to suffering.

"It took me three years to whittle these definitions [of love and belonging] from a decade of interviews. Let's take a look.

"**Love:** We cultivate love when we allow our most vulnerable and powerful selves to be deeply seen and known, and when we honor the spiritual connection that grows from that offering with trust, respect, kindness, and affection. Love is not something we give or get; it is something that we nurture and grow, a connection that can only be cultivated between two people when it exists within each one of them—we can only love others as much as we love ourselves. Shame, blame, disrespect, betrayal, and the withholding of affection damage the roots from which love grows. Love can only survive these injuries if they are acknowledged, healed, and rare.

"**Belonging:** Belonging is the innate human desire to be part of something larger than us. Because this yearning is so primal, we often try to acquire it by fitting in and by seeking approval, which are not only hollow substitutes for belonging, but often barriers to it. Because true belonging only happens when we present our authentic, imperfect selves to the world, our sense of belonging can never be greater than our level of self-acceptance.

"One reason that it took me so long to develop these concepts is that I often don't want them to be true. It would be different if I studied the effect of ... bird poop on potting soil, but this stuff is personal and often painful. Sometimes, as I turned to the data to craft definitions like the ones above, I would cry. I didn't want my level of self-love to limit how much I can love my children or my husband. Why? Because loving them and accepting their imperfections is much easier than turning that light of loving-kindness on myself."[2]

It seems as though we humans have this impossible choice. We can risk becoming vulnerable, "open to attack," rejection, and exclusion by expressing our true selves, or we can *not* risk. We can cover up, we can fit in, we can go along.

This dilemma has been recognized throughout history. The Classical Greeks carved their motto in stone, "Know thyself," meaning, *do not bend to the opinion of masses*. And, they executed Socrates for asking questions. In the 1700s, the Enlightenment *philosophes* talked about "Man in Nature" versus the social person and how we've made tradeoffs and compromises to live in society, which is so unfortunate because the natural, independent man was seen as pure, wise, and virtuous. A century later, Carl Jung talked about the *anima* versus the *persona*, the

---

[2] Brown, Brené (2010-09-20). *The Gifts of Imperfection: Let Go of Who You Think You're Supposed to be and Embrace Who You Are* (p. 26-27). http://goo.gl/GpVgjx

fundamental self versus the constructed, social self. Freud's version of it was the id of drives tempered by the ego of social norms. In the 1950s and '60s, the French existentialists talked about alienation, anxiety, conformity and self-expression.

Because we so crave acceptance and need to belong we will sometimes settle for creating a fake persona that seems acceptable. But if you buy into this split of either protecting yourself vs. risking everything, then you must create a character, an avatar that fits into the group and is accepted by the family, church, or club. But even if that pretend person is accepted by your community, you still don't experience belonging, do you? Who is it that **seems** to belong? It's not you. It's a confidence game, a "con." A fraud.

Looking from the other perspective, if others in our company, our neighborhood, or our nation are not expressing to us who they are in their hearts, how could we belong to anything true since **they** are not being authentic with **us**? If our friends must pretend certain beliefs, suppress opinions, or act a particular way in order to meet our standards ... their hearts are not accepted—there is no real friendship in that relationship, just accommodation.

Joseph Campbell, the mythologist, said in an interview,

> "What if we choose not to do the things we are supposed to do?
> "The principal gain is a sense of an authentic life. It may be a short one, [Laughter] but it is an authentic one, and that's a lot better than those long lives full of boredom [and pretense].
> "The principal loss is security in the respect of the community. But you gain the respect of another community, the one that is worth having the respect of."[3]

In preparing for this talk I thought of an incident ... no, more of an ongoing charade from when I was in high school. I went to an all-male Catholic high school. When I label it that way you immediately think you know a lot about it—and you are probably right. [Laughter]

There was this one boy who was small and blond and artistic, with a soft voice ... and *everybody*

---

[3] *Myth & the Body* - A colloquy with Joseph Campbell by Stanley Keleman, Center Press July 1, 1999 http://goo.gl/faOrz7

made fun of him. We all gave him a hard time. I participated, because it was easy to be part of that mean game. To go along, to fit in. No, I did more. I excelled at belittling, labeling, and excluding him.

I look back on that now and realize that the thing that most irritated my adolescent self about this boy was, no matter how many of us rejected and ridiculed him, he just kept on being artistic and walking the way he walked and talking the way he talked. Why did he get away with being who he was while the rest of us were using him to pretend to fit in? It took courage for him to come into that unwelcoming, critical environment every day for four years. I was only brave enough to cover myself by playing the accepted game of gay-bashing.

I had a poster in my room the whole time I was in high school and college, but I never really got the point until much later in life. It was a picture of Lincoln with the quote, "To sin ... by silence, when they should protest, makes cowards of men."

Do not shrink from saying, "I will not sit silently while you talk that way about people of ... a particular race ... or gender ... or **me** that way." To be polite and compliant in the face of hatred, bigotry, or coldness is cowardly, not courteous. To be silent in such circumstances diminishes me, of course, but reticence also insults the people around me, because I have judged them incapable of learning and growth, unworthy of my insights and values.

This is widely acknowledged as the central issue of high school but it doesn't end when we graduate. It just moves underground. We get better at reading the room, avoiding conflicts, hiding, or pretending. Or, someone comes along who seems to be genuine and fully expressed; a Luke Skywalker, Lady Gaga, or Barack Obama, and we say, "Yes, that person breaks the mold." "We like that." "We need to follow her." Or, "Be more like him." And often that becomes just another clique, a litmus test of belonging, the sort of situation lampooned by Monty Python in "Life of Brian." Brian, bewildered and irritated at being venerated by the mob, tells them he is not special, that they are individuals who don't need to follow him, that they can follow their hearts. But the mob merely chants Brian's words, verbatim, in unison. "Yes, we must think for ourselves." [Laughter]

This story plays out again and again in offices and homes and churches. Shame is so frightening, belonging so vital, it seems that we are continually confronted with this dichotomy of choice. We must either risk being emotionally vulnerable and open to attack and rejection, or we cover up, we fake, we pretend, we stifle ourselves. We go along to get along.

But is this an *impossible* conflict? Do we *have* to accept this *Sophie's Choice* between one or the other? To be phony or to be lonely, to belong or to be real? Well, maybe not. I firmly believe that the world is made up of two kinds of people. There are those who divide the world into two kinds of people and those who don't. [Laughter]

Maybe we can step away from this dichotomy. Cut the Gordian knot. We all, each of us, have unique internal natures with yearnings, values, and concerns that we want to express into an accepting environment. We are all ... always ... coping with society, with groups that might not accept us as we are, and we will all encounter people that we are uncomfortable accepting as *they* are.

Perhaps we can choose to act in accordance with a concern for everyone's authenticity. To have the strength to express our unique selves **and** learn behaviors that smooth our own path to acceptance without suppressing anyone else's authenticity.

That's courage.

Maybe we can go even further. Let's adopt a conscious practice of accepting other people when they behave in a way that we don't understand or are uncomfortable with of listening in a generous manner, as you are right now. Let's resolve to welcome authenticity from others, to practice compassion for the difficulty our friends and family have with expressing their genuine selves to us.

Compassion. Such a great word. It means *with* passion. *Passion* is the Latin word for *suffering.* **Com**passion means to be with the other person's suffering.

I read a wonderful article in *Harper's* magazine titled, *The Separating Sickness: How leprosy teaches empathy by Rebecca Solnit.*[4]

She tells the story of the last facility in the U.S. for people with leprosy, now called Hansen's Disease. I learned that it is caused by a bacteria that destroys the nerves which produce pain. Sounds good, right? A life with no pain. But we need pain. Pain is a vital information that helps us modify our behavior to avoid bodily damage, wounds that can cause the broken, infected fingers and scars that we associate with Hansen's Disease.

Surgeon Paul Brand wrote a book about his time at the clinic and the title says a lot, *The Gift of Pain.*[5] He wasn't just talking about what a gift pain is to a person with the capacity to feel his own hands and face. Dr. Brand's experience working with the sick and suffering taught him that compassion, being **with** another's pain, was a gift, too.

---

[4] http://goo.gl/edMC61

[5] http://goo.gl/fNFk7h

The article in *Harper's* summarized his insight this way:

> "... ***shared pain is central to what it means to be a human being***, but we are a society that values the anesthetic over pain. We hide our prisons, our sick, our mad, and our poor; we expend colossal resources to live in padded, temperature-controlled environments that make few demands on our bodies or our minds. We come up with elaborate means of not knowing about the suffering of others **and of blaming them** when we do.
>
> "*Choosing not to feel pain is choosing a sort of death, a withering away of the expansive self.*"

You don't have to work in a leper colony to practice courageous compassion. Often, all it takes is the willingness to slow down long enough to let the other person speak. You don't need to take away the pain or solve the problem. The gift of attention with compassion is valuable and healing by itself.

That's **generous** courage, action from our heart that **generates** courage for the other. That's what en-courage means, to give courage to someone. Put courage in them so they might be more in touch with their own hearts, maybe even more open to other people's hearts.

We can have compassion for others, sure. Let's try some selfish courage. Will you exercise compassion and love for your *own* struggles and reluctance to step out, to say what's really on your mind and in your heart? I **want** you to have selfish courage, for your sake, but also for mine. Because I want to know the real you. I do.

Back now to that discussion I mentioned earlier, when the woman from Holland asked a room full of executive coaches, "Why be vulnerable if it means 'being open to attack'?" After listening to everyone have their say, what I took away was, for me, an insight that leads me to specific practices. "Vulnerability is choosing my actions with the knowledge that other people participate in my life."

"Vulnerability is choosing my actions with the knowledge that other people participate in my life."

I should point out that I was raised with a very American, John Wayne, do-it-yourself, individualistic ideal of manhood. I gave that worldview a good try and after a few decades I had to admit that, if that approach was going to work out, it would have by then. [Laughter] So I had to look at something else and I realized that everything I wanted in life required the actions of other people.

You can't hide when you need other people. Pulling away from pain or risk, or responsibility, just leaves us alone and incomplete; fitting in but missing out. Further, not only did I need people to make my life worthwhile, my life was *best* when other people needed and accepted my participation in their lives. That's a very vulnerable place to be; needing and being needed. Worse, needing to be needed. Lots of opportunities to fail, to be rejected, to fall short.

But, still, we can create those rare moments when, through familiarity and acceptance, we have made peace with the voice in our heads, the ceaseless inner voice that repeats our flaws and chants our fears. When the roar of self-doubt becomes a meaningless background hum like the air conditioner that you know is still running but it is not running you. In those moments of freedom, I can turn my attention to the people around me, look past the accommodations they make to fear and self-doubt, and listen for what comes from their hearts, their core.

In those moments,
we might have the courage to say:

You can believe that
your heart is safe with me.
Because I've trusted you
with my cautious heart.

When I can do that for someone
who then reveals their true nature to me,
whenever anyone hears what is in my heart,
what we feel is love.

As I do, as you do,
as *we* do,
right now.

Part Three

How to BE in Courageous, Genuine Relationships

Choosing the topic for this new chapter of *The Courage to Be in Community* was not difficult. Listeners and readers gave me clear feedback about what was most needed. They all wanted to know what specific actions to take—or behaviors to stop—to foster courageous, genuine relationships for themselves and those closest to them. Several key questions emerged:

- What can I do in my day-to-day life to deepen relationships?
- How can I feel comfortable with people of different backgrounds, tastes, and values?
- How do I help others feel safe to share their lives with me?
- What habits might I establish to reduce loneliness and build community?

The challenge in writing this chapter was not in finding enough material but in paring down the plenitude of powerful practices that I learn, teach, and apply every day as an executive coach to business owners and their teams.

I learned these things the hard way because I am not a "natural" at nurturing friendships and fostering community. Not nearly. I had to learn friendship as an adult, through frustrating and humbling experience.

I suffered the pain of loneliness and alienation as a child and well into adulthood. I had an exceptional talent for generating irritation where I needed cooperation. I applied anger where curiosity would have served better. Doors were closed to me because I hurled the bomb of righteousness when the healing balm of compassion would have opened doors. I still struggle but I am grateful for the support of authors, coaches, and the many people I have encountered who were more patient and kind with me than I was with them. Sometimes, I am also grateful for the people who were not patient or kind but instead gave abrupt, often unwelcome feedback that spurred me toward a better path in life.

In this short chapter I cannot share everything I have learned but, after much review, consideration, and application; I have chosen to focus on three practices that have opened up a new world of more open communication for me:

1. **Be** humble
2. **Be** curious
3. **Be**ware the second person

BE HUMBLE

Some of the most effective coaching consists of bringing to mind a teaching that sounds obvious, that we seem always to have recognized as true and useful, yet which we fail to rigorously apply in day-to-day life. Many of these have become so familiar that we have entombed their practicality in cliché: "Treat others as you would be treated." "To err is human, to forgive divine." *Et cetera.* If only we respected such wisdom by consistently applying it, our lives and communities would be better.

But we do not. Our frequent failure to consistently be our best selves is an "obvious" aspect of being human that inspires my first recommended practice: Be Humble.

No one knows what you know. You have a unique set of experiences, opinions, and emotions. Even when in the same room, each person notices different features. Even when two people share the same facts, they may have different reactions to those features. These reactions happen instantly and just below the level of normal awareness; we seldom give a thought to this leap from perception to conclusion. It is just how we operate. Most of us, most of the time are examining the world "through a glass, darkly." Everyone *knows* this, though few apply it. We typically assume that our own narrow, distorted, and personal view of the world is the clear, objective, and universal reality.

It is easy to see how this plays out in relationships. My first, unconsidered reaction to people who disagree with me is not to reevaluate my opinion of the *situation* but to lower my opinion of *them*. They must be wrong, ignorant, augmentative, or—if I feel charitable—distracted, inattentive, or tired. I "help" them by explaining my position.

Humility would help more.

I am working to develop the habit of responding to disagreement or even disconnection with humble curiosity. Instead of teaching, I seek to learn. Instead of defending my position, I visit theirs. Maybe I will see something useful from their unique perspective. Even if I do not change my opinion, I improve the relationship, because people prefer having their ideas respectfully received rather than being corrected or rejected.

> We all love being heard, because being heard is a big part of being loved.
>
> —Tony Mayo

BE CURIOUS

At a reunion for graduates of a coaching program, we were asked to share the biggest change in our lives since the training. I said, "I have given up my hobby of mind reading. I am no longer satisfied by my assumptions about what other people are thinking and feeling. Now, I ask and listen."

Everyone wants to matter, to be significant to others. The first step to letting the people around you know that they matter is to invite them to share what is going on in their heads. The key is to ask with genuine curiosity. I care what the person is thinking and feeling. I thank them for being frank and sincere. I adjust my response based on what they say. I share my own thoughts and feelings.

> Intimacy is present when the conversation in our heads matches the conversation in our speech.
>
> —Julio Olalla

When we invite someone to sincerely share their feelings and opinions, we risk hearing unwelcome words. When that happens, it pays to be curious and ask gently what the person meant by what you heard. It is also very useful to start from the assumption that they intended no harm, are not being critical, and are merely doing their best to cope with the situation at hand.

> It's not the things you don't know, what gets you into trouble.
> It's the things you do know, that just ain't so.
>
> –Will Rogers

More on genuine curiosity at
http://tiny.cc/morecurious

Beware the Second Person

My genuine relationship advice to "Beware the second person" does not mean that you should be afraid of the person with whom you are speaking. Instead, I am suggesting that you be wary of using the second person pronoun, "you." Using the second person is sometimes correct, of course, but it is also the hallmark of two common speech patterns that undermine genuine relationship.

One corrosive use of "you" occurs when someone expresses his or her opinion of how another person *is*. Every time I tell anyone how they are, what they think, or what they did to me, my words are layering another filter between me and the facts. This distorts reality and confines the other person within the boundaries of my opinion. Sentences that pass judgment on a person with labels such as "rude," "unreliable," "foolish," etc. "pass a sentence" on that person, punishing him or her to serve that "term." This is called objectifying because it treats a human as if they were an inanimate object with fixed, unchanging characteristics. This objectification makes it harder to see the person as alive, that is, learning, adapting, and growing.

The second way the misuse of the second person pronoun "you" often hurts our friendships, marriages, and working relationships occurs when we try to make our own reactions and opinions seems obvious and universal, even seeking to avoid personal responsibility for what we are saying. Instead of complaining, "When people leave dirty dishes on the kitchen counter for hours, you naturally feel like no one cares about how hard that makes cooking," try, "When people leave dirty dishes on the kitchen counter for hours, *I feel* like no one cares about how hard that makes cooking." See the difference? Here is another contrasting pair. "When your husband flips the channels while you are trying to explain a problem with the kids, you know he just doesn't care." Rather, "When *my* husband flips the channels while *I* am trying to explain a problem with the kids, *I feel* like he just doesn't care."

Two things happen when we make the shift from the universal yet nonspecific "you" and "your" to the personal "I" and "my." One, it relieves the listener from the burden of agreeing or disagreeing with your generalization. A person talking about their own, unique experience is the *de facto* expert; there is no reason for me to take a position on whether it is true. It is the speaker's experience and that is all that matters. Second, the speaker in the first person is no longer blaming the other for forcing anything on him or her; the speaker is simply sharing how he or she felt about what happened. It is the shift from, "You made me angry by changing the subject," to, "When you brought up a new subject, I noticed that I felt angry." One is an accusation; the second is a confession. One evokes defensiveness, the other encourages a calm, constructive response. Accusation incites aggression. Confession calls for compassion.

Mindful use of the first person *I* avoids both dangerous uses of *you*. Share your feelings, interpretations, and reactions responsibly by using I. This does not demand agreement, it just accesses a response, and that makes for a conversation that fosters genuine, alive relationships.

> One friend, one person who is truly understanding, who takes the trouble to listen to us as we consider our problem, can change our whole outlook on the world.
>
> —Dr. Elton Mayo

I have one more suggestion, perhaps the most powerful practice of all:

BE KIND

Just as I often fail to act in accordance with my best knowledge and highest values, I am wise to remember that each isolated action or failure to act by my neighbor or co-worker may not represent her best knowledge and highest values.

When I fall short of my aspirations, I am quick to explain and excuse myself because of fatigue, haste, stress, traffic, etc. Always, my excuses claim some form of, "That's not me; it was just an unfortunate circumstance. Don't hold it against me." When I observe my spouse or the store clerk do something I dislike, I am just as quick to use it as proof of how they really are. And, to use their disappointing action to excuse or explain myself the next time I let that person down.

This common behavior is tempting because it gets us off the hook of blame and responsibility for the moment but over time its effect is corrosive to relationship. Indulge in "It's not me, it's them" frequently and the people around us learn that we are not safe to be near, that eventually we will give them a failing grade. Instead, when someone seems to be letting you down, be humble about your own blamelessness, be curious about what the other person's intentions and circumstances may be, beware of passing a sentence on the second person when first person responsibility would be more nurturing. In short, be kind.

> Be kind, for everyone you meet is carrying a great burden.
> —Philo of Alexandria

http://tiny.cc/morekind

I regret that so little of what I have learned about building courageous relationships could be summarized in this short document. I am sure that I could write an entire book or even three on this topic—and I plan to. Watch for their publication on my Amazon Author Page or by subscribing to my free email newsletter and podcast. If you cannot wait for my next books, and I do not see why you would, here are some resources I recommend that are available right now.

A very clear and assessable book is the widely used *Crucial Conversations: Tools for Talking When Stakes Are High.* http://tiny.cc/cc-book

I gave several classes based on this material at my church and the participants produced inspiring results at work, with teenaged and adult children, as well as in their marriages. I hope you will, too.

If you are primarily interested in improving your marriage relationship, you can do no better than to attend an Imago Workshop™ with your spouse, such as *Getting the Love You Want: The Couples Weekend Workshop* http://tiny.cc/imagocouples.

Imago was developed by the man who has been Oprah's most frequent guest, Harville Hendrix. You might want to start with his book, *Getting the Love You Want: A Guide for Couples*, 20th Anniversary Edition, http://tiny.cc/imagobook, but there is no substitute for actually doing the exercises with your spouse and other couples in a workshop assisted by a skilled facilitator.

> It can be very hard to get along with the people you love.
> It is much harder to get along without people to love.
>
> —Tony Mayo

Another book I can highly recommend, one that emphasizes work and business relationships, is *The Communications Catalyst: The Fast (But Not Stupid) Track To Value For Customers, Investors, And Employees*, http://tiny.cc/comcat. The very first day I learned the methods in this book I witnessed them being dramatically employed by an expert. It happened at an international conference for employees and customers of a large executive coaching organization. While I was in class, the president of the company found himself at the podium in a ballroom filled with very angry customers, some of whom interrupted his speech with loud complaints. He had planned to give a bland speech of welcome and self-congratulation but found himself in a fight for the future of the company. Some longtime clients even stood to announce their resignation and stormed out of the ballroom.

The chairman of the company's board of directors recognized this as an emergency. He interrupted our class on *The Communications Catalyst* to confer privately with the instructor. After the chairman left, our instructor told us that he had been asked to facilitate an ad hoc reconciliation meeting after our class.

It was quite a learning experience for me to go directly from the classroom and downstairs to a live fire demonstration by my instructor. He implemented a textbook approach, just as he taught us to do, and, in the course of ninety minutes, guided about fifty people from contention to cooperation, from hot anger to warm amity. By the end of the meeting, everyone was clear on their common values, eager to improve cooperation between company and client, and people in both camps had committed to specific follow-up actions. It was amazing and inspiring.

For more on improving business relationships visit my blog, Top Executive Coaching.

- A recipe for better conversation, with video and a summary poster.
  http://tiny.cc/concontract
- How asking questions, even in response to a question, helps improve communications and relationships.
  http://tiny.cc/morecurious

- My 12 step program to shake a dangerous dependence on avoiding confrontation. http://tiny.cc/toughtalk

- How groups agree. http://tiny.cc/groupagree

There are lots more material there on the specifics of business life and the business of life in general. If you want to be sure to see my newest material, you may subscribe for free to my blog, podcast, or newsletter.

Would you like more people to hear this message?
Spread the word by posting your review to Amazon at

http://tiny.cc/TonySermon

About the Author

Tony Mayo is an executive coach to owner operators of mid-sized businesses. His work with CEOs and their teams on complex issues of strategic importance includes: one-to-one coaching, design and facilitation of strategy and alignment retreats, and enduring peer-consulting teams of top executives from different organizations.

He is a master of analogy and anecdote whose illustrations are as likely to come from his studies of brain science, high energy physics or eastern philosophy as from his years of management and sales in high-technology. Whether speaking from a platform, coaching one-to-one, or facilitating a workshop, Tony maintains a laser focus on his goal of helping people realize their dreams.

Tony earned his MBA from the University of Chicago at age twenty-one, after three years of high school and three years in college. He immediately started a business that he sold in 1982.

Tony has worked with Arthur Andersen & General Electric, founded boot-strap and venture-backed start-ups, and taught at the college, graduate, and executive levels. Tony is the sole inventor of US Patents 6,678,663 & 7,930,209. His most important activities today are family fun, working with top executives, and total health. All with one unifying purpose: to promote workplaces of humanity and prosperity where people can be productive and satisfied.

Originally from Rhode Island, he lives in Reston, Virginia with his wife and three children.

Learn more about Tony and read more of his work on his Amazon Author Page at:
www.amazon.com/author/tonymayo
his blog at: **www.TonyMayo.com**
or Facebook page: **www.facebook.com/Tony4CEOs**

BEFORE YOU GO...

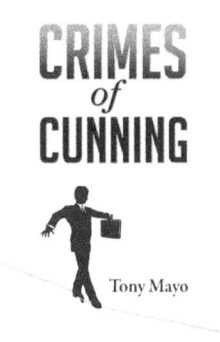

You may be interested in Tony's novel. *Crimes of Cunning: A comedy of personal and political transformation in the deteriorating American workplace.*

Fast-paced, funny, and smart. This novel puts you into the world of a young MBA striving to succeed at a famous high-tech company. Brash and confident yet comically inept, Tony clashes with colleagues, clients, and even his biggest supporters. He fires his most loyal employee, derails the career of his only friend, and nearly destroys his young marriage before transforming from chilly corporate collaborator to empathetic executive coach. Laugh and learn as his clients turn criminal, corporations collapse, and compassion triumphs.

A veteran executive coach draws on his years inside Arthur Andersen, Wall Street, and MCI to share a moving story that explains why your 401k shrank, your house is underwater, and your job stinks. The comedy and conflict illustrate management methods and personal practices that can improve your career and deepen your personal relationships.

http://tiny.cc/2cunning

Design Credits

Cover photograph by Tony Mayo

Author photograph,
front and back cover design
by
Tony Mayo
&
Sonja Hope Mayo

Inner Layout and Design
by
Andrea Leljak

Available in Kindle format from Amazon at
— http://tiny.cc/TonySermon —
and as an audiobook read by the author on
Audible.com, Amazon, and iTunes.
— http://tiny.cc/hearsermon —
Available in hardcover & paperback
wherever books are sold, worldwide.

CPSIA information can be obtained
at www.ICGtesting.com
Printed in the USA
LVHW101859290722
724726LV00002B/50

9 781941 466087